This book is dedicated to

Mimi

"My little grandmother
from Chile"

Tales from my

Grandmother's

Kitchen

First published in 1998 by Absolute Press
Scarborough House, 29 James Street West,
Bath, Somerset, England BA1 2BT
Tel: 01225 316013 Fax: 01225 445836
email: sales@absolutepress.demon.co.uk

© Jessica Gibson, Simone Alyward
© Illustrations Nigel Noyes

The rights of Jessica Gibson to be identified as author of this
work have been asserted by him in accordance with the
Copyright Designs and Patents Act 1988

Printed by The Cromwell Press, Trowbridge

ISBN 1 899791 91 4

Tales

from my

Grandmother's

Kitchen

Jessica Gibson

Design and Concept
Simone Aylward

Illustrations
Nigel Noyes

Contents

Conversion Tables

Weights

Throughout this book all measurements are imperial. Mimi feigned total disinterest in metric, and if you wish to enter into the spirit of it you can do the same.

However the conversions are here if you need them - just remember to never mix imperial and metric in the same recipe.

1 oz	=	25 gms
2 ozs	=	50 gms
3 ozs	=	75 gms
4 ozs	=	110 gms
5 ozs	=	150 gms
6 ozs	=	175 gms
7 ozs	=	200 gms
8 ozs	=	225 gms
1 Lb	=	450 gms

Conversion Tables

Volume

(imperial cups)

1/2 cup	=	1/4 pint	=	150 ml
1 cup	=	1/2 pint	=	275 ml
1 1/2 cups	=	3/4 pint	=	425 ml
2 cups	=	1 pint	=	570 ml
2 1/2 cups	=	1 1/4 pint	=	725 ml
3 1/2 cups	=	1 3/4 pint	=	1 litre
4 cups	=	2 pints	=	1.2 litre

*L*et me tell you about my grandmother Mimi. My memories of her are inextricably linked with extravagant food, colourful tales and eccentric advice. I picture her now, in the drawing room of her London house, holding forth on the folly of health foods whilst cutting thick slices of Rich Chocolate Cake. Her careful English was full of luxuriously rolled r's from her Chilean upbringing:

"Salad is for rrrabbits, my dahhlings!"

Her blue eyes were set deep into a small heart shaped face. Her grey hair was always worn in an elegant French chignon and her face was devoid of make-up apart from a touch of powder and lipstick. Unlike my other grandmother her cheeks had no prickles! Her skin was pale and soft, like paper. I loved kissing it and smelling her scent of face powder and Chanel No 5.

Mimi came to England just before the first world war, still only a teenager. She met my grandfather, William Ross-Munro whilst working in a London hospital, although her favourite version of their courtship involved a dropped glove on a South American ocean liner. They married shortly afterwards and went on to have three children; Ian, my mother Carmen, and Colin. Her life was not without tragedies though and she lost Ian and Carmen at early ages.

I was seven when my mother died. From then on, Mimi became a momentous influence in my life, as grandmother, mentor, mother figure and friend. Through her my sense of identity grew and I learned about my mother and her childhood. Mimi's sunny personality helped heal the pain of my loss and she kept me entranced with her stories and advice whilst she cooked in the kitchen.

Her reference was the hundreds of recipes she had collected over the decades, each scripted in her careful hand, with occasional lapses into Spanish. These were not plain homely dishes but rich extravagant creations lathered in cream, often dosed in brandy and full of occasion. For better or worse, Mimi taught me to appreciate the most exquisite dishes and how to be obsessed with what delicacies to eat next; the rewards of cooking!

It was whilst visiting relatives in Santiago a few years ago that the idea of a cookery book took root. Everyone had a favourite Mimi story that seemed to transcend the barriers of age, class, language and sex, and still somehow lead back to the kitchen.

I have so many stories and recipes now, it's hard to know where to start. But let's begin by calling the family to table.

The Family Table

my uncle
Colin

my aunt
Jan

Mimi
my grandmother

Me

Emma
my best fri

Mrs. Neale
the home help
my Chilean cousin
my brother
George
Ian
Tara
my sister
Antonia
my sister
Tony
Nona
my father
my paternal grandmother
red squirrel

"Class
somehow
made up
for everything"

Mimi's mother's maiden name was Aguirre and Mimi would often remind us of our famous lineage. Aguirre, one of Pissarro's lieutenants, was responsible for founding La Serena in the sixteenth century and as a young girl Mimi would promenade around his statue in the main square. Pissarro himself went on to conquer and unite the whole of Peru.

In 1912 Mimi came over to England with her mother and 14 year old brother Hermann. Her parent's marriage was not a happy one and her father was more than content to be left behind on his farm outside La Serena in Chile.

Upon arriving in London, Mimi began voluntary work at a local army hospital. William, my second grandfather-to-be, was soon to be a patient there.

A Scottish architect, William was travelling in Egypt when war was declared and he promptly joined up at the nearest Australian garrison. After each day of drills, he returned to his room at Shepheard's Hotel, the grandest in Cairo, where he was required to use the side door because of his private's uniform. After a brief and shocking campaign, he was gassed in France. Whilst he managed to woo Mimi during his convalescence, his health always remained fragile.

In 1915 at the age of eighteen Mimi visited her prospective in-laws at their presbyterian home in the Isle of Skye. She was immediately disgraced when found playing the piano on Sunday afternoon, a sin not far below blatant heresy.

News of her presence spread and at 2 am one morning the household was woken by the Highland Light Infantrymen who arrested Mimi on suspicion of being a German spy. Her incarceration was shortlived as she won freedom with the help of a Spanish dictionary and boastings of diplomatic connections.

Her in-laws' parsimonious spirit was reflected in their bland and unappetising cooking. From then onwards Mimi referred to them as "those awful old puritans" and never quite found the time to visit them again.

After Mimi and William married he became the London Manager of the New York City Bank. My mother Carmen was born in 1926 and being a girl, William doted on her. Times became hard as the world fell into depression. In 1929 his London branch made a paltry eighteen pounds and the whole bank went bust.

William switched to stockbroking in the thirties and he and Mimi enjoyed the pre-war prosperity. But during the war years more stresses followed for William, precipitating a breakdown in 1943 from which he never fully recovered.

My mother and her brothers Ian and Colin grew up with Mimi and William in Chelsea. Like many mothers Mimi found it hard to let go of her children as they matured, particularly as the oldest, Ian, went to war never to return.

Mimi rather disapproved of my mother's choice of husband ("such a plain man dahhling but he has good posture") and was so incensed with Colin's wedding plans that she persuaded William to boycott it. On the *morning of the wedding, Mimi changed her mind but insisted on wearing a black hat throughout the day. Willliam, being a man of principle, was left at home.*

I sometimes wonder if Mimi made an eleventh hour pact with Colin before the wedding, because for the next thirty years she lived in a flat directly beneath Jan and Colin in a large house in Chelsea sharing innumerable meals, pre-dinner drinks, holidays and a succession of cleaning ladies.

For many years Mimi looked after William as an invalid and she was left a widow in 1960.

Mimi slipped easily into her self appointed role as head of the family and was known as the "iron fist in the velvet glove". Though she was never slow to lavish love on us all she would not hesitate to point out our failings. A favourite saying for my sister and I was "You may not be real beauties, but you have class". Class somehow made up for everything.

Mimi's 'bible' was her dog-eared black leather-bound folder in which she carefully recorded all her recipes. This was hidden away in one of her kitchen drawers together with odd bits of twine, scissors and newspaper clippings. My favourite drawer was for special occasions and contained old paper serviettes, birthday candles and tin pastry cutters in the shape of hearts, stars and an assortment of different animals.

It all begins in
Mimi's Kitchen

Her kitchen was old fashioned and humble in contrast to the sophisticated dishes which spilled out of it. The floor was covered in a warm coloured faux marble linoleum and most of the available space was taken up by a sturdy formica topped table where Mimi cooked, read and ate when not entertaining. Next to the table was a cold, stone tiled larder full of Fortnum & Mason tea caddies and faded tins of biscuits decorated with fluffy kittens or puppies.

Canned peach halves in syrup lined the shelves, as Mimi was not a lover of fresh fruit unless it was bananas baked in the oven, served with lashings of fresh cream. Commercial sauces were also hidden in the larder to be used for cooking only. However my brother Ian used to sneak the tomato ketchup onto the table when Mimi wasn't looking. Work surfaces were covered with different kinds of cooking implements - pudding bowls stacked in diminishing sizes, ornamental cake and muffin trays and an old pair of scales with measuring weights. Far better than lego was the game of neatly building these weights one above the other without letting them collapse. In one corner stood an old mincer which Mimi would clamp onto the edge of the table when she made Ian's favourite 'corn beef hash'. As a result the side of her table had permanent indentations.

with some appetising appetisers

Mimi's butler's sink overlooked her walled back garden. This was a small city enclave paved with stones surrounded by flowering plants and miniature fruit trees. In the centre stood a little stone cherub with water spouting from its pouting lips. When the weather was fine we would have tea in this secluded and leafy retreat.

Green Pea Soup

(serves 6)

*T*his heart warming soup with its distinctive
flavour and bright colouring would make its
first appearance in early spring when peas were at
their most succulent. I remember sitting cross legged
on the big formica kitchen table shelling peas for
Mimi, popping the bright green peas from their
shells, but wary of any squirming maggot poking its
head out at me! But preparation is half the fun of
cooking, so invite a
friend over and
exchange gossip
whilst
making
light of
this task.

4LBS FRESH PEAS	**LETTUCE LEAVES**
1/4 CUP FLOUR	**A SPRIG OF PARSLEY**
1/4 CUP BUTTER	**SALT**
6 CUPS CHICKEN STOCK	**1 CUP OF CREAM**
1 SLICED ONION	**2 EGG YOLKS**

Cook the shelled peas for six minutes, retaining the cooking water. Puree or process until smooth.

Melt the butter in a large pan over a low heat and blend in the flour, cooking the roux until golden.

Add a little of the liquid in which the peas were cooked and the chicken stock.

Cook liquid until smooth. Add onion, lettuce leaves, parsley and salt. Simmer for 20 minutes.

Press through a sieve and add some more of the pea juice. Return to the pan and stir in the pea puree.

Re-heat gently, adding the cream and egg yolks. Be careful not to boil.

Delicious served with hot crusty bread.

The Old Rectory

*M*y childhood and early teens were spent in a
small eighteenth century village called Ewhurst -
about 15 miles outside Guildford. Our house
was The Old Rectory, a large rambling building set beside
a listed barn. This barn was balanced precariously on stone
mushrooms which no doubt were there for the practical
purpose of keeping rodents at bay. For us children it provided
an underground world of tunnels and secret rooms where
we would play endless games. On rainy days we were as dry

as denned foxes smug in the knowledge that no one knew where we were. We would tighten our breath on catching a glimpse of Mimi's slender ankle as she called us into lunch or tea on one of her frequent visits to Surrey.

The garden was dominated by a towering cyprus tree and backed onto the cemetery where my mother was buried.

To reach my bedroom at the top of the house I had to climb three flights of stairs. From there it was a short run down a corridor flanked with doors where the boilers were kept. They made a constant 'schwoo schwoo' sound like ghosts whispering to me. Two more steps led up before turning the corner to my bedroom with my father's dressing room adjacent. There were three additional bedrooms belonging to my siblings but after Ian and Duncan went to prep school, then Harrow they remained empty apart from the school holidays. It was around this time that my imagination ran riot.

Before going to bed I would have to check every piece of furniture in my room for lingering ghosts. My father's dressing room was full of shadows. I would quickly flick through his row of suits before scampering into bed. Once there I would stuff the bottom of the bed with all my toys and then snuggle right down under the covers. No subsequent creaks or groans from the old house would entice me to raise my head above the covers until morning!

Avocado Soup

(serves 6)

*A*vocados were one of the few fruits that Mimi was fond of. However, though she never counted the calories in sweets I can hear her now warning me about the fat content in avocados, which I adored. This recipe is divine but extremely rich so only a small serving is needed.

The sour cream can be replaced with single cream if you wish.

CHICKEN STOCK (STRONG)

1 LB OF CUT PEELED POTATOES

1 1/2 LB OF THINLY SLICED LEEKS

1/2 PINT OF MILK

SALT & PEPPER

1/2 PINT OF SOUR CREAM

2 MEDIUM SIZED AVOCADOS

CHIVES TO GARNISH

Put the cut and peeled potatoes and the thinly sliced
leeks into a pan and cover with the chicken stock.
Simmer gently until the vegetables are
soft enough to purée through a sieve.
After puréing add the milk
and some salt & pepper as required.
Chill thoroughly.
Once chilled add the sour cream and stir in the flesh
of 2 medium sized avocados (crushed by hand).
Serve in thoroughly chilled glass bowls
and garnish with finely scissored chives.

*A*fter our mother died Mimi's influence on our lives became stronger than ever. She visited us at The Old Rectory for weeks at a time ensuring we were well fed but despairing of the endless flight of au pairs complaining of "little savages". Six months later Daddy married Ann and evenings spent sitting in a row in the bath guessing the

identity of a stepmother were over.

Since the Old Rectory could accommodate

Little Savages

us all there was no question of having to move. Fiona, Sally and Duncan, (my new step sisters and brother) were allowed to choose their new bedroom even if it was already occupied. I suppose the logic behind this was that it would compensate them for the loss of their former home but it caused havoc. Ian and I gave up our bedrooms easily enough but dislodging Tara wasn't so easy. In the end she stayed put, Daddy having decided that an all out war with her was worse than "taking on a whole army".

Rows between siblings and step siblings erupted on a daily basis. One minute Tara and Sally would be amicably riding their ponies and the next minute spitting venom over whose knickers belonged to whom.

Though fiercely protective of Ian and I from any outside criticism Tara went through a stage of leaping on me without the slightest warning, pulling my hair and yelling "We didn't want you, we wanted another boy". At seven years younger I was no match for Tara but I do remember chasing Ian around the garden with a bamboo switch, lashing out at him until he burst into tears.

During these emotional upsets, if Mimi was staying we all welcomed her sympathetic ear in the comforting warmth of the kitchen.

Lentil Soup with Red Wine *(serves 6)*

4 CUPS OF BEEF OR VEGETABLE STOCK

1 1/2 CUPS OF RED WINE

2 CUPS OF WASHED LENTILS	**2 STALKS OF CELERY**
2 ONIONS	**DRIED THYME**
6 SLICES OF BACON	**MARJORAM**
2 TBLSP BUTTER	**1 BAYLEAF**
1 HAM BONE	**2 POTATOES (PEELED)**
1 CARROT	**TARRAGON VINEGAR**

FRESH CHERVIL AND CROUTONS TO SERVE

Soak the washed lentils in 1 quart water
for 1/2 hour, (keeping the water).
Chop the onions and bacon
and sauté in the butter until the onions are golden.
Stir in the lentils with the water,
the stock and 1 cup of red wine.
Add the ham bone, carrot, celery (diced),
bay leaf and a pinch of thyme and marjoram.
Simmer for 45 minutes.

Add the potatoes (diced) and the remaining 1/2 cup
of red wine and cook until the potatoes are soft.
This will take about 45 minutes.
Remove the ham bone and the bay leaf
and press the soup through a sieve.
Just before serving reheat the soup
and add 1 tblsp of tarragon vinegar.

Sprinkle with chervil and serve with croutons.

Denture dreams

For a long time, although I slept regularly in Mimi's bed, I had no idea she wore dentures. But then one night when I was around six years old my sleep was disturbed by a dream. Mimi was no longer in my room and instead, in the shadows a terrifying creature with wild grey hair and no teeth sat at Mimi's dressing table rubbing cream into its sunken face.

The next morning I told Mimi about the witch I had seen. She reassured me that the witch had gone now - Mimi would look after me. In future she kept her teeth close to hand in her nightglass so she could fish them out at short notice!

There was one time however when Mimi had to do without her dentures for the day whilst they were being refitted. The lower part of her face was now collapsed and rubbery and sitting at her kitchen table she seemed somehow smaller and more vulnerable.

I can remember Ian and I swallowing laughter at lunch whilst poor Mimi began grinding away on her food with such an effort you would have thought she was cracking bones. She kept on laughing herself, holding her hand coyly in front of her mouth like a young girl and telling us to stop being so unkind otherwise a similar fate might befall us as that which happened to her friend Maria at school.

Poor Maria had been rather a plain girl and unlike Mimi had few suitors. Finally when she was about to give up hope of ever marrying a young man called to her parents house one afternoon. Whilst her mother left the room to prepare tea his feelings overwhelmed him and he bent forward kissing her in a very ungentlemanly way.

Unfortunately for poor Maria she had recently undergone some intricate dental work and several of her false teeth lodged at the back of his throat. By a stroke of good fortune Maria's neighbour happened to be a doctor - otherwise the hapless young man may well have suffocated to death. His ardour cooled, and once the story spread her fate was sealed and Mimi told us poor Maria died an old maid.

Walnut Soup

(serves 6)

6 OZ SHELLED WALNUTS   **I LARGE CLOVE OF GARLIC**

1/4 PINT CREAM   **SALT**

2 PINTS LIGHT STOCK   **BLACK PEPPER**

Crush the walnuts and garlic to a paste with
a little of the stock, pounding well.
Incorporate the rest of the stock slowly until
the mixture looks like single cream.
Sieve into a saucepan and slowly bring to the boil,
adding salt and freshly ground black pepper to taste.
Add the cream and serve straight away.

Kipper Soufflé

(serves 4)

1/2 LB KIPPERS (COOKED)

2oz BUTTER　　**2 EGG YOLKS**

1oz FLOUR　　**3 EGG WHITES**

1/2 PT MILK　　**PEPPER**

Heat the butter in a large pan, add the flour and cook for about 2 minutes. Next add the milk gradually to form a smooth sauce and cook for about 5 minutes until thickened. Chop the cooked kippers into small pieces and mix into the sauce.

Add the egg yolks one by one.

Whisk the egg whites until stiff and mix in gently.

Pour into a 6" soufflé dish and cook for about 30 minutes at 200^0c, 400^0f or Gas mark 6.

Paté Maison

(serves 6)

*R*ich but light with a sophisticated flavour, this paté makes a good picnic dish for hot summer days. Mimi used to spread it on crusty bread with lashings of unsalted butter.

As children we would pack up a picnic hamper with these and other goodies and take it across the road to the park. Whilst we'd lie on a blanket on the grass, Mimi would preserve her dignity by sitting on a bench. Somehow eating in the park was not considered 'lowly' although eating publicly in the streets would have been out of the question.

Sometimes Jan and Colin would join us on the weekend and we would pile into one of Colin's sports cars for a jaunt into the country. Although Mimi always seated herself in the front, getting into the car elegantly had its problems. "Such a selfish choice of car dahhling". She was much happier seated in my cousin's 2CV from which springy height she could view the world with regal composure.

8OZ OF CHICKEN LIVERS	**3 SHALLOTS OR 1 ONION**
3OZ OF BUTTER	**1 CLOVE OF GARLIC**
1 TBSP FRESH PARSLEY	**SALT AND PEPPER**
PINCH OF DRIED THYME	**1 DSP OF BRANDY**

*Finely chop the shallots or onion,
crush the garlic and soften in 1oz of butter.
Add the chicken livers and sauté for 5 minutes,
or until the livers are thoroughly cooked.
Sprinkle with the chopped parsley,
thyme and salt and pepper and cook for 1 minute.
Cool a little, chop roughly and pound well.
Stir in 2oz melted butter and 1dsp of brandy.
Mix well and pack in a mould and chill.*

Delicious eaten with hot toast.

Chilean Fish Soup

(serves 4)

*T*his authentic Chilean soup is so chunky you could serve it as a main course with lots of warm crusty bread. If you like your food fiery, add more of Mimi's hot chilli sauce - Aji de Color.

1 1/2 lbs Firm White Fish

1/2 lb Small Clams, Tinned or Fresh

1 tsp Aji de Color (Recipe on Page 40)

1 lb Tomatoes	**Salt**
2-3 Potatoes	**Pepper**
1 Onion	**2 cloves of Garlic**
1 Carrot	**1/2 tblsp Butter**
1 Glass White Wine	**Juice of 1 Lemon**

If using fresh clams, place in a little water and cook
briefly over a high heat until the shells open.
Reserve the broth.
Melt the butter in a pan and sauté
the sliced onions and crushed garlic until soft.
Roughly chop the tomatoes,
slice the carrots and add to the pan.
Simmer gently for 10 minutes.
Add the white wine, a glass of water,
aji de color, reserved broth from clams
(or tinned clam's juice), sliced potatoes
and salt & pepper.
Bring to the boil, cover and simmer gently
until the potatoes are almost cooked.
Add the fish, cut into chunks,
together with the clams, and continue cooking
until fish and potatoes are cooked.
Just before serving, stir in the lemon juice.

HYDE PARK
KENSINGTON ROAD
KNIGHTS BRIDGE
BROMPTON ROAD
HARRODS
SLOANE STREET
BROMPTON ORATORY
NATURAL HISTORY MUSEUM
CROMWELL ROAD
CADOGAN SQUARE
SOUTH KENSINGTON
MICHELIN BUILDING
SLOANE SQUARE
PETER JONES
SLOANE AVE
FULHAM ROAD
CHELSEA
PIMLI
KINGS ROAD
CHELSEA ROYAL HOSPITAL
TEDWORTH SQUARE
CHELSEA PHYSIC GARDEN
EMBANKMEN
THAMES
RIVER
WORLDS END
CHEYNE WALK
ALBERT
BATTERSEA PARK

*T*hough I lived at The
Old Rectory until I was
fourteen years old, I spent
numerous weekends as
a child visiting Mimi in
Tedworth Square off the Kings Road.

At Mimi's house bought shop cakes
were taboo and the arrival of my brother
and I with our weekend suitcase was
always greeted with open arms and the
expected three tier chocolate cake still
warm from the oven.

When my parents moved to Kent I was
sent to boarding school and saw Mimi
only on exeats and during the holidays.
In my teens I moved in with Mimi thrilled
at the prospect of living in London.

Aji de Color

(Chilean hot sauce)

Yaya Marshall and Mimi met at convent school in La Serena. Yaya was a colourful character famous as much for her amorous dalliances as her witty asides. At the tender age of fifteen her brother preserved her honour by shooting her first lover in an attempt to preserve her innocence, though by all accounts Yaya was keen to lose it! Her capacity to shock was still in evidence when visiting friends at their country house one rainy weekend years later. Sweeping into the living room she pronounced:

"When there's weather like this there's only two things to do and I don't play cards!"

Mimi always said that Aji de Color reminded her of Yaya, hot and spicy and ageing well.

I oz Dried Red Chilli Flakes

I clove Crushed Garlic

1/3 cup Olive Oil

1/2 cup Boiling Water

1/2 tsp Salt

Soak the chilli flakes in the boiling water
for about half an hour, and then drain the
soaking water into a screw top jar.
Pound the chillies, garlic and salt in a
pestle and mortar, (in batches if necessary)
using a little of the water to break them down.
Add the chilli mixture to the jar
and pour in the olive oil.
Shake well before using.

Store the sauce in the refrigerator,
with a little olive oil on top to maintain freshness.

Empanadas
in their Honour

Mimi was just about as interfering as me with regard to matchmaking. However she was a pragmatist with money high on her list of priorities.

She regularly invited marriageable girls of wealthy pedigree to dine or take tea with her at Tedworth Square. Somehow my elder Chilean cousin George always got invited as a last minute addition on the pretence that he was in the area.

Mimi allowed him the starter and main course to get acquainted with her choice before asking him to clear the table. After a final few inquisitive questions alone with the hapless girl Mimi would follow George out to the kitchen and get his opinion. Poor old George never shared Mimi's taste - the wealthy girls were always too dull and any that sparked his interest had committed some terrible faux pas like wearing a mini skirt, drinking from the finger bowl or, worse still, asking for the toilet instead of the loo!

There was only one time that she did get it right. The girl in question was a skinny Australian full of vivacity and for once the conversation was not stilted. After the main course George began to clear the table and waited for Mimi in the kitchen who turned up soon enough. George eagerly expressed his interest to which she replied in dismay, "But she has no money dahhling!" Deciding to overlook this shortcoming Mimi started giggling and plotting with George. During dessert it turned out that the Australian girl had no intention of staying in England. When Mimi realised this she said "Oh no dear. That simply won't do. If I had known you were going back I would never have invited you to dinner!"

George eventually insisted on inviting his own dinner dates to Mimi's and their private half time kitchen whisperings became more heated, particularly when Mimi accused George of "baby snatching" girls that looked as young as 15.

As time slipped by she began to get desperate and on one occasion invited two Chilean girls to tea, making Empanadas in their honour. They bored George so rigid that after a short time he began to look at his watch and make his excuses to go. Mimi sensed an unsatisfactory end to her afternoon so immediately threw in an angina attack. It was decided that the girls should leave instead. Poor George was given a sound ticking off but they quickly settled down with a glass of sherry to catch the end of Coronation Street.

I always wondered why Mimi never paired me up with George. I suppose the match didn't meet her standards, although I never found out which one of us fell short!

Empanadas

(makes about 18)

1 LB OF MINCED LOIN OF PORK

1 TSP OF AJI DE COLOR

(CHILEAN HOT SAUCE - MIMI'S RECIPE IS ON PAGE 40)

2 TBSP OF OIL	**BLACK PEPPER**
6 LARGE MINCED ONIONS	**SALT**
A HANDFUL OF FLOUR	**3 HARD-BOILED EGGS, SLICED**
2 TBSP OF STOCK	**3 TBLSP RAISINS**
1/2 TSP OF CUMIN	**2 TBLSP BLACK OLIVES**

Empanada dough

8 OZ OF LARD	**15 TBSP MILK**
3 LBS FLOUR	**2 EGG YOLKS**

Fry the minced pork in 2 tbsp of oil and when it is half cooked add the minced onions, and fry for a while longer. Add the stock, aji de color, cumin, salt and pepper to taste, and a handful of flour. Remove from the heat, stir in the olives and raisins and put to one side.

Making the dough...

Rub the lard into the flour

(make sure the lard is at room temperature).

Add the egg yolks, and gradually add the milk

until you have a dough consistency.

Do not knead too much.

Roll out the dough in a couple of batches.

You will find the dough is quite flexible,

and should be rolled out thinly.

Cut around a saucer to make circular

empanadas, and fill each one with the

meat mixture and slices of hard-boiled eggs.

Rub a little milk around the edges

and seal into pasty shapes.

Cook in a hot oven, 220°c, 425°f or Gas mark 7,

until golden brown.

Skin like a
Withered Apple

Nona was my grandmother on my father's side. She was the youngest of five girls and had stopped speaking to all of her sisters over the years due to some unfortunate remark or other. When Daddy gave her the news of her eldest sister Florrie's death she merely yawned and said "Oh really!"

Nona and Mimi were the only grandparents I knew, as my grandfathers had either disappeared or died a long time before. Mimi was round and cuddly, but Nona had ossified into something really scary. Even scarier, she lived next door to us in the other half of the Old Rectory.

Nona's part of the house was like a mausoleum - cold, with stone floors and shrouded antique furniture in rooms that were out of bounds to children.

Nona herself only inhabited a few of the rooms. Even these weren't exactly homely. She would sit in her drawing room on an old chinz sofa facing the empty fireplace like some dissipated queen down on her luck but still rigid backed with pride. She had a thin prickly face and skin like a withered apple. I used to dread kissing that cheek and inhaling her peculiar smell - decay mixed with something sweet and cloying.

There were times when we would be sent round to say hello. As we tapped on her drawing room window the sight was always the same - the back of a bony skull covered in sparse grey hairs. "Nona" we would call "we've come to say hello". Without turning her head she would reply in clipped tones "Not today thank you".

Salad
is for
Rabbits

D *ieting and health foods were concepts that Mimi kept firmly at bay. Any humble salad ingredient was heavily disguised in a lavish dressing.*

As she grew frail she would sometimes have to stay in a nursing home whilst Jan and Colin were away on holiday. If a plain salad was served she would shrivel her nose in disgust and pronounce, "Salad is for rabbits and the civilised classes will always be well dressed!"

Salsa Amaulla

*T*his is a quick and delicious salad dressing, which Mimi loved to serve poured over new boiled potatoes and sprinkled with chopped chives.

She would chop the remaining white of the hard boiled egg over the potatoes whilst reminding us to "Waste not want not".

2 EGGS
I TSP DIJON MUSTARD
I TBLSP WHITE WINE VINEGAR
2 TBLSP EXTRA VIRGIN OLIVE OIL
SALT & PEPPER

Mash the yolk of one hard boiled egg together with the mustard, and when smooth mix with a raw yolk. Beat up well and gradually add the oil and vinegar, beating until the sauce thickens.
Season with salt & pepper.

Mayonnaise Andaluz

1 1/2 CUPS OF STIFF MAYONNAISE MADE WITH LEMON

1 TBLSP WORCESTERSHIRE SAUCE

3 RED SWEET PEPPERS　　**1 TBLSP COGNAC**

3/4 CUP DOUBLE CREAM　　**1 TSP POWDERED PAPRIKA**

1 TSP CRUSHED ICE　　**1 TSP CAYENNE PEPPER**

1 TBLSP TOMATO KETCHUP　　**SALT AND PEPPER**

*Use good quality egg mayonnaise -
homemade is best but ready-made will be fine.*

*Whisk the double cream with the teaspoon of
crushed ice. Put the red peppers through a fine
mincer, and stir into the cream.*

*Mix in the mayonnaise, tomato ketchup,
Worcestershire sauce, cognac, cayenne pepper,
paprika, and salt and pepper.*

*Delicious served with green salad or seafood,
or as a sauce for that great classic,
the prawn cocktail!*

Green Goddess Dressing

1 (2 oz) TIN OF ANCHOVY FILLETS

3 TBLSP DRY VERMOUTH OR WHITE WINE

1 CLOVE OF GARLIC	**1 SMALL ONION**
1/2 PINT MAYONNAISE	**6 LARGE SPRIGS OF PARSLEY**
2 TBLSP TARRAGON VINEGAR	**1/4 PINT SOUR CREAM**
1 1/2 TSP LEMON JUICE	**SALT AND PEPPER**

This dressing is typically rich, and makes 3/4 pint.
Make half quantities if you don't need that much.

Put anchovy fillets, onion, garlic and parsley
through a fine mincer or food processor.
Add the remaining ingredients and mix well.
Cover and chill for several hours
to blend the flavours.

This goes very well with green, chicken or seafood
salads. It's also delicious over poached salmon.

Mimi and the subject of sex

*L*ike her attitude to food, Mimi had a sensual outlook on life. She would never consider openly discussing the subject of sex, but was certainly not naive. Men were never to be trusted and she was fond of giving me ambiguous warnings, her favourite being "Never sit on a man's lap dahhling, strange things may happen!"

She had a sixth sense tuned towards unseemly behaviour as my eldest sister, Antonia found out.

She was entertaining a young man in her bedroom when late at night she heard to her horror the tap tap tap of a walking stick echoing on the marble floor outside her room. Hurriedly bundling her guest into the cupboard she turned to see Mimi silhouetted in the doorway saying:

"Dahhling, I've just had a terrible dream about you, are you alright? Now you come sleep with Mimi we'll keep each other company".

Perhaps she got part of this astuteness from her reading material. As her fingers began to lose their dexterity and she could no longer embroider she turned more and more to reading. My uncle was often the provider of new material. His raunchy taste in books has always been a subject of amusement and they provided Mimi with an opportunity to tut tut in mock disgust and horror. However, when it was suggested that the book be exchanged for something more seemly she would always insist that "Once started, every book, no matter how bad, should be finished".

Siesta Time

Siesta time would often find Mimi in a contemplative mood. She'd lie propped up on her queen bed whilst I'd mooch around, fiddling with the silver brushes on the dressing table and peering at the myriad of photos underneath its glass top.

If she was feeling 'comme ci, comme ça' life wasn't too bad but she was in need of a little fortifying reminiscence. I loved to hear stories about her girlhood and Mimi positively trilled when describing what a looker she had been in her day. In her bottom drawer she kept a reminder of her youthful brilliance; a long ponytail of auburn hair which she had cut off when she was eighteen. I remember clipping it to my springy sad example of a ponytail and looking in the mirror as I swished my head from side to side like a movie star.

If however she was feeling 'piano' her thoughts would turn to death and only by determining that everything was in order could she regain her equilibrium.

"Dahhling" she'd say "could you get my box down from the wardrobe for me, I want to look at something".

It was a large cardboard box filled with pale pink tissue paper. Inside was a rose coloured filmy nightdress with a matching fine wool bedjacket lined with chiffon and feathers. Mimi would pat it and say "remember dahhling this is what I want to be buried in. Make sure I'm wearing it when I go".

Then she'd make wheezing noises into her handkerchief, point to her heart and set her eyes rolling towards the bedside drawer where she kept her angina pills. After I placed one under her tongue the crisis would pass. I'd leave her with her  glasses perched jauntily on the end of her nose, happily reading another chapter of some racy novel.

At around 6pm Mimi would have a glass of vermouth or, in the event of Chilean relatives coming over, a Pisco Sour. Living only upstairs, my uncle Colin was duty bound to join her and her guests.

She would always tidy herself up beforehand, powdering her face and adding a quick spray of Chanel No 5, her favourite scent. She

Dutiful Drinks

had a drawerful of this perfume as Colin would buy it for her whenever he was away on business.

At The Old Rectory there was a similar ritual with Daddy also expected to have a drink with Nona every evening. He would fortify himself with a swift G and T with Mummy beforehand and walk over, rather wearily.

He always said that it was his
war experience that helped him
to down Nona's drinks with
incredible speed. "Have another
drink darling" Nona would say to which he would
invariably reply "I won't thank you very much, I have to
be getting back". The response was always the same -
"Yes to that wife of yours I expect!"

Pisco Sour

3 PARTS PISCO (A CHILEAN SPIRIT)

I PART FRESH LEMON JUICE

DASH OF SUGAR SYRUP

CRUSHED ICE

SALT

Rub the rim of a glass with lemon to moisten,
then dip it in salt.
Shake the remaining ingredients together
and pour into the glasses.

Cheese Savouries

4 oz Plain Flour

4 oz Butter

2 oz Finely Grated Cheddar Cheese

1 oz Fine White Breadcrumbs

a Pinch of Salt and Cayenne Pepper

Rub the butter into the flour, and add the breadcrumbs, salt, cayenne pepper and cheese. Bind into a pastry and roll out on a floured surface until fairly thin. Cut out small biscuits with the pastry cutter of your choice and place on a greased baking tray. Cook for 10 - 15 minutes at 200°c, 400°f or Gas mark 6.

If Mimi was pressed for time she would serve these with drinks straight from the oven.

If, however time allowed, or she was entertaining to impress, she would sandwich the little biscuits together with a smooth Welsh Rarebit mixture. You can find this recipe on page 100 - just delete the Worcestershire sauce to make it Welsh instead of Yorkshire!

The Main
Event

*L*ate afternoon would find Mimi setting
the table in her small dining room - its
sombreness accentuated by dark green
walls. A chandelier hung over the large
oak table that dominated the
room. On the walls hung drawings of birds, newly shot
and in the throes of death with their fragile heads flung
back and broken.

...twenty minutes to lay a beautiful table

An extract from The Woman's Feature of The Times circa 1955

Set the cloth with the design
exactly in the centre of the table.

Space the places out evenly -
a minimum of 24 inches for each, leaving
each guest enough elbow room.

Lay the centre-pieces. The candlesticks,
salts, sugar sprinkler and mustard
and pepper containers, and the large jade seal
that is always used for the middle of the table.

Place flowers, in small Waterford glass bowls,
at either end of the table.

Place the spoons, knives, forks and glasses
and finally...

The napkins, simply folded to set off the
lace design, between each place setting.

Petit Filet Elizabeth

(serves 4)

For more than twenty years Mimi kept detailed lists of all the dinner parties she gave. This included not only the names of her guests but what they ate and drank.

When writing to my relatives in Chile for help on some of Mimi's recipes I was able to jog their memories by reminding them of the last dinner they had with Mimi. This was one of her favourite dinner party dishes.

The recipe combines the sweetness of redcurrant jelly with the tartness of French mustard. Together with the cream and sherry this makes a sauce fit for kings.

the main event

1 LB FILLET OF BEEF	**1 TSP FRENCH MUSTARD**
1 TBLSP FLOUR	**4 OZ MUSHROOMS**
1 TBLSP BUTTER	**1 GLASS SHERRY OR PORT**
1 TBLSP OIL	**5 FL OZ DOUBLE CREAM**
1 CHOPPED ONION	**SALT**
1 TBLSP REDCURRANT JELLY	**BLACK PEPPER**

Slice the beef into thin strips,
season with salt and pepper and dust with flour.
Sauté in the butter and oil, quickly adding
chopped onions and mushrooms.
Cook for 3 or 4 minutes,
drain off the fat and add the sherry or port.
Cook for a further 2-3 minutes,
until reduced a little, take off the stove
and add the redcurrant jelly, mustard and cream.
Adjust seasoning, but do not reboil.

Serve with new potatoes and a green salad.

Oyster Loaf

(serves 6)

I LOAF OF WHITE BREAD - UNSLICED LOAF TIN STYLE

I PT WHITE SAUCE (SEE RECIPE BELOW)

8 OZ MUSHROOMS   24 OYSTERS

I TBLSP LEMON ZEST   SALT & PEPPER

for the white sauce

I 1/2 OZ PLAIN FLOUR

2 OZ BUTTER

1/2 PINT OF MILK

1/2 PINT OF STOCK

SALT & PEPPER

To make the white sauce

Melt the butter, remove from heat and stir in the flour. Put back on the heat and cook for a couple of minutes, adding the liquid very gradually, stirring quite vigorously all the time. When all the liquid has been incorporated cook the sauce over a low heat until thickened. Season with salt & pepper.

To assemble the loaf

*Cut about 1 1/2 inches from across the top of the
loaf of bread. Scrape out the inside,
and process or grate into breadcrumbs.
Place the oysters into the hollowed loaf.
Slice the mushrooms and stir into the white sauce.
Mix the lemon zest, 3 tblsp of the breadcrumbs,
the white sauce, and season with salt and pepper.
Pour over the oysters until the loaf is full.
Put the lid back on, and place a weight on
the top to hold it down without breaking it.
Bake in a preheated oven for 30 minutes
at 180ºc, 350ºf or Gas mark 4.*

Cut into slices and serve with a green salad.

Beefsteak, Kidney and Oyster Pie (serves 6)

"**P**astry needs cold hands and a warm heart," was one of Mimi's favourite sayings and this pie combining the richest of pastry and savouries is certainly heart warming.

Sometimes we were allowed to help with the pastry and would clumsily cut out our own decorations.

I still remember the feeling of absorption and contentment in handling dough and Mimi's blissful satisfaction when she lifted her masterpiece from the oven, cooked to golden perfection and filling the kitchen with an unforgettably mouth-watering aroma.

the main event

2 LBS CHUCK STEAK   **2 CHOPPED ONIONS**

8 OZ OX KIDNEYS   **6 OZ SLICED MUSHROOMS**

12-18 OYSTERS   **BEEF STOCK**

WORCESTERSHIRE SAUCE   **1 OZ BUTTER**

HEAPED TBLSP FLOUR   **SALT & BLACK PEPPER**

Basic suet crust pastry;

12 OZ SELF-RAISING FLOUR

6 OZ SHREDDED SUET, (PACKET SUET IS FINE)

Cut the steak into cubes and kidneys into slices.
Season with salt & pepper and brown quickly
in the butter, adding the onion. Stir in the flour
and cook for a moment. Add oysters and their
juices together with the mushrooms and enough
stock until the sauce resembles thick cream.
Season with worcestershire sauce to taste.
Transfer to a covered casserole and pre-cook in
the oven for an hour at 170⁰c, 325⁰f or Gas mark 3.

making the pastry...

When the filling is nearly ready, sift the flour
into a bowl, sprinkle in the suet and mix lightly
with your hands to distribute it evenly.
Add some iced water and continue mixing
until you can use your hands to bring it
together to form a smooth dough.
Leave for 5 minutes, then roll out immediately.

Pour the pie filling into a 2 - 2½ pint pie dish,
and cover with your pastry lid.
Turn the oven up to 200°c, 400°f or Gas mark 6,
and bake pie for 30-40 minutes until
the pastry is cooked to golden perfection.

*M*imi was always very particular about good manners and etiquette. Even now as adults we all remember with fondness her smacking our lazy elbows resting on the table at dinner time

Aeroplano, Aeroplano

exclaiming "*Aeroplano, Aeroplano!*" This imaginative picture of our arms resembling the wings of a plane did more to improve our table manners than a sharper remonstration would have done. If, however a sterner threat was required to put a curb on our naughtiness she would threaten to come back from the dead "to tickle our toes".

Pastel de Choclo

(Corn Pie, serves 6)

1 Whole Chicken Breast

12 Black Olives, Chopped

2 Cans of Creamy Kernel   **2 Hard-boiled Eggs**

Basil Leaves   **1 tblsp of Raisins**

The Piño

(a Chilean word meaning 'seasoned filling')

1-2 tsp Aji de Color (recipe on page 40)

1 lb Ground Beef   **2 tblsps Stock**

1 tbsp Flour   **1/2 tsp Cumin**

2 Onions   **Salt & Pepper**

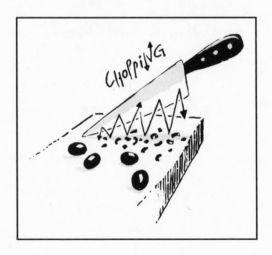

Make the Pino

Fry the beef in oil and when half cooked add the
finely chopped onions. Fry for a while longer.
Add the stock, aji de color (add more if you like it hot),
cumin, salt & pepper and flour.
Remove from the heat
and put to one side.

sprinkling

To complete the dish

Chop the chicken breast and fry until cooked.
Put the prepared piño in a layer in an oven dish,
add the chicken, sprinkle with chopped olives,
raisins, torn basil leaves and slices of boiled eggs.
Lastly, spread the creamy corn kernels in a layer
over the top, and bake in the oven for 20 minutes at
180°c, 350°f or Gas mark 4.

TEARING

Congratulations on your Engagement

ara met Bill when she was fourteen years old. He lived about a mile away from us at Pitch Hill with his father and siblings in a beautiful sprawling house called Rapsley. Since Mummy died Tara had been spending most of her time there. It was the mid 1970's and Rapsley was like a commune, full of hippies advocating free love and growing their own marijuana. Bill's father had Parkinsons disease and exerted little control.

I was around ten at the time and during summer would often go to Rapsley after school to have a swim in the pool. Waves of anxiety would sweep over me because I knew Tara and her friends scorned wearing costumes and mine would be confiscated. Hovering by the pool I used to cling onto my towel for dear life whilst Tara laughed at my shyness and everywhere around me young men and women were jumping into the pool starkers!

Around this time Tara and Bill announced their engagement and I was ecstatic at the prospect of becoming a bridesmaid. Mimi insisted on meeting Bill but knew that Tara would never acquiesce without my help. I decided immediately to stage the Sound of Music in their honour as it was the only record in my collection! The play was to be set on Mimi's huge bed allowing easy access to the crucifix hanging above. Cushions were laid out on the floor as front row seats. Since it was my sister getting married I was to play Maria whilst my best friend Emma had to play all the minor parts.

Tara and Bill were duly sent their invites and a date was set for the play. Rehearsals consisted of two afternoons of screeching sopranos, giggling and fluffing of lines.

I remember little about the play itself - Suffice to say Tara and Bill called off their engagement within a few days.

Burning
our Bridges

O ne rainy Sunday morning shortly after my eighteenth birthday Mimi decided that she was going to take a break from cooking and announced that my friend Emma and I were to make Sunday roast. There was to be no set menu, no other visitors and we had full use of her kitchen.

We settled Mimi into the drawing room with a sherry and the Sunday Mail whilst we started peeling muddy potatoes. After a couple of hours messing about we arrived at the dining table with a huge mound of mushy vegetables and an upside-down roast chicken. Mimi insisted on turning it over to reveal the soggy pale breast skin topped with a flat pear shaped burn from the pan. After struggling to free a couple of slices of pink inner flesh she discovered some cleverly hidden stuffing - a wrinkled plastic giblet bag.

Although everything had a strange aftertaste, we persevered. It was the quietest meal I remember at Mimi's house. Afterwards she pronounced that our cooking was so dreadful that we would never make good wives or mothers. Luckily she was never told that somehow I had thickened the gravy with icing sugar!

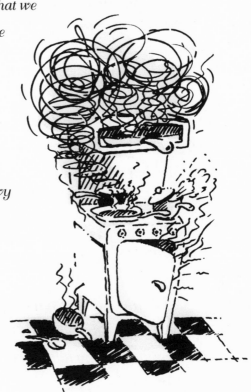

Chicken stuffed with Prunes & Chestnuts

(serves 6)

A LARGE CHICKEN (OR TURKEY)

1/2 TSP NUTMEG, CINNAMON AND GROUND CLOVES

15 PRUNES SOAKED OVERNIGHT IN TEA

1 1/2 LBS PORK   **3 TBLSP BREADCRUMBS**

3 RASHERS BACON   **2 TBLSP CHESTNUT PUREE**

2 HEAPED TBLSP PARSLEY   **A GLASS OF PORT**

Chop the prunes, mince the pork and the bacon and
mix all ingredients together except for the port.
Season well with salt and pepper. Stuff into the bird,
butter lavishly all over and lay it on its back in a
roasting tin. Cook in a preheated oven at 200°c,
400°f or Gas mark 6, for 20 minutes per pound and
20 minutes extra, basting occasionally.
You can turn up the oven temperature for the last
20 minutes to give a nice crisp skin.
When cooked leave the bird in a warm place to rest
before serving. Meanwhile boil up the pan juices
with a glass of port to make a sauce
and serve on the side.

*I*n the early evenings, I used to watch TV in Mimi's drawing room sitting on a little tapestry stool whilst she stroked the curls from my face. That room was close to my greedy heart. Mimi had told me that everything in there would be mine when she was gone. I soon learned that each grandchild had been promised

Close to my greedy heart

a certain room, although it was not until years afterwards that I realised that there were many more grandchildren than rooms.

I still have the little tapestry stool though, because Mimi had written my name underneath.

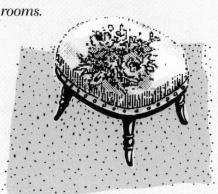

18th Century Devonshire Pie

(serves 4)

1 1/4 LBS LAMB OR MUTTON CHOPS

3 GREEN APPLES	**2 MEDIUM ONIONS**
1 LEVEL TSP MACE	**16 UNSOAKED PRUNES**
1 LEVEL TSP CINNAMON	**1/3 PT MEAT STOCK**
1/2 FRESHLY GRATED NUTMEG	**SALT & BLACK PEPPER**

Basic short crust pastry;

8 OZ PLAIN FLOUR

2 OZ BUTTER OR MARGARINE

2 OZ LARD OR DRIPPING

PINCH OF SALT

COLD WATER

First make the pastry...

Sieve the flour and salt into a mixing bowl. Quickly and lightly rub in the fats, using your finger-tips. Try to keep everything as cold as possible. Mix in enough cold water to form a soft dough (about 4 tblsp). Cover and put in the refrigerator to rest for 20 minutes.

Meanwhile cut the lamb or mutton into slices
and chop the onions. Saute the onions
and add the meat, quickly frying to seal
and brown slightly. Put to one side.
Cut the prunes into small pieces,
peel and core the apples, and cut into quarters.
Take a 2 pint pie dish and arrange the meat,
apples and prunes in layers, sprinkling with
the spices and salt and pepper as you go.
Roll out the pastry to about 1" wider all round
than your pie dish. Trim this edge off and stick
onto the rim of your pie dish. Now moisten
with water and roll on your pastry lid,
sealing around the edges with the back of a knife.
Make two small holes to let the steam out.
Cook in a pre-heated oven for about 1 1/4 hours
at 170⁰c, 325⁰f or Gas mark 3.

This is nice serve with puréed root vegetables
(potatoes, pumpkin or parsnips) and spinach.

Very Common Behaviour

*B*eing a woman of privileged background Mimi never had to seek paid work. I was not going to be so lucky but Mimi's advice of "Whatever you do don't ruin your hands dahhling", left things pretty much up to me.

My working life started off shakily. I brought an end to a very lonely four month stint as a French au pair in Paris when I discovered I had put on two stone from my diet of chocolate croissants. I then worked for a while in the condoms department for Boots in the Kings Road where my friend Karen worked in the cosmetics department. Punks were constantly consulting Karen as to the best eyeliner and me for black ribbed condoms.

My career was quickly becoming a taboo subject when at the age of twenty-two after completing my first degree I had an interview with Macdonalds. Mimi associated Macdonalds with eating on the streets - very common behaviour. Typically the reality of the sparky nylon trousersuit and the subservient undertones of the staff training video made a second day of my Macdonalds career too painful to contemplate.

Spiced Red Cabbage with Caramelised Chestnuts

(serves 6)

1 SMALL RED CABBAGE	**1/4 TSP CINNAMON**
6 BACON RINDS	**1/4 TSP MACE**
1 LARGE COOKING APPLE	**1/4 TSP CLOVES**
1 LARGE ONION	**1/4 TSP GROUND PEPPER**
GRATED RIND OF 1 ORANGE	**1/4 TSP ALLSPICE**
2 TBLSP BROWN SUGAR	**1/4 PINT OF RED WINE**

Caramelised Chestnuts

3/4 LB WHOLE CHESTNUTS

2 OZ BUTTER

1 OZ SUGAR

1/2 TO 3/4 PINT STOCK

*Using a heavy lidded pan, melt the bacon rinds
then remove. Shred the cabbage thinly,
chop the onion and apple and put into the pan.
Add the red wine, sugar, orange rind and spices.
Stir well, cover with a tightly fitting lid
and cook in the oven for 2 1/2 hours
at 130⁰c, 275⁰f or Gas mark 1.*

Meanwhile make the caramelised chestnuts...

Remove the skins from the chestnuts.

Melt butter, add the peeled chestnuts,

sprinkle with sugar and let them brown

before adding the hot stock.

Cover lightly and cook gently

until the liquid is absorbed - about 3/4 hour.

Uncover and leave the chestnuts over

a gentle heat until sticky and shiny.

Fold into the red cabbage mixture once ready.

This dish is delicious served with all meats,

particularly roast pork.

Mimi liked to serve this with good sausages

from Harrods food emporium.

Lambs Kidneys in Brandy

(serves 4)

Mimi simply adored kidneys and this was one of her favourite recipes that she would serve up as a quick lunch or early supper in front of the television.

Amazingly enough for small children, my brother and I shared Mimi's delight in kidneys! We were of course ignorant of the essential trimming of fat and hoses!

8 Lambs Kidneys	**1 tblsp Fresh Parsley**
1/2 Glass Dry White Wine	**1 dsp Dijon Mustard**
2 Shallots	**2 oz Butter**
1 Clove of Garlic	**Salt**
2 tblsp of Brandy	**Black Pepper**

Remove any fat from the kidneys and cut into quarters.

Finely chop the shallots and parsley.

Melt the butter in a pan over medium heat,

add the shallots and the clove of garlic

(whole but crushed), and sauté for 2-3 minutes.

When sizzling add the kidneys with salt,

pepper and the mustard.

Mix well, letting the kidneys brown,

turning from time to time.

Warm the brandy, add it and set it alight.

Add the wine, cook to reduce for 2 minutes,

remove the garlic and sprinkle with parsley.

Serve with boiled potatoes, and a full red burgundy.

A French Lesson

Mimi was fluent in several languages and made sure her children were fluent in at least two by sending them to the French Lycée in Chelsea. Though I took French lessons at school, mastering languages did not come easily to me. I had a good ear for accents and my trick was to talk really quickly so that the listener would not notice my execrable verb construction. Giving up briefly on French I tried Spanish to capitalise on my Chilean blood but Mimi's face would register complete incomprehension at my efforts.

Turning back to French Mimi organised yearly exchanges with French girls my age. The first year produced a very tomboyish girl with whom I climbed trees and played croquet but the following year a tall strawberry blond materialised. Against her I felt woefully inadequate. My spirits rose when I learnt the colour at least was straight from a bottle. After two hours in the bathroom with a bottle of peroxide I emerged downstairs to gasps of genuine horror. My skin looked jaundiced against the orange fuzz of my hair and my brothers were delighted to bestow on me a new nickname - 'helmet head' to add to 'thunder thighs'.

Mimi's response was a sad shake of the head coupled with "Ah dahhling, you have lost half of your looks."

That summer also remains vivid in my memory for gastronomic reasons.

Chantal, on top of her beautiful looks also happened to be a fantastic cook, and earned Mimi's respect with her recipe for Tarte à la Moutarde. Perfect for hot summer days served with a light salad and warm crusty bread, it is quick and easy to make. Mimi was impressed enough to include it amongst her recipes.

" *Il faut Souffrir d'etre Belle "

*One must suffer to become beautiful

Tarte à la Moutarde

(serves 6)

for the pastry	*for the filling*
10 OZ PLAIN FLOUR	**3 TBLSP DIJON MUSTARD**
2 EGG CUPS OF OIL	**6 OZ GRUYERE CHEESE**
2 EGG CUPS OF HOT WATER	**6 LARGE SLICED TOMATOES**
1/2 TBLSP BUTTER	**BLACK PEPPER**
PINCH OF SALT	**GREEN SALAD TO SERVE**

Put all the pastry ingredients into a plastic box
with a lid, and shake until they form a ball.
Roll out on a floured surface and line a flan tin.
Spread the pastry with the mustard
and sprinkle on half the grated gruyère.
Layer on the sliced tomatoes,
and top with the remaining cheese.
Add a good grating of black pepper,
and place in a preheated oven,
200°c, 400°f or Gas mark 6, for 35 minutes,
or until golden brown.

*N*ona's first husband and Daddy's father was Claude De Vesci Gibson. He was mostly English but mixed with just enough Spanish to have contributed the "De Vesci".

Claude had no money but Nona was wealthy thanks to her father. They were married and in 1917 Daddy was born. Nona told him that she used to see Zeppelins over the coast as she pushed him in his pram in St. Margaret's Bay.

Zeppelins over the Coast

His sister Mavis arrived 20 months later, eleven days before the Armistice. Nona threatened to call her 'Makepeace' but mercifully opted for a more conventional name.

Shortly after their marriage in 1919 they decided to emigrate to South Africa and take up farming. They left on an ocean liner which is where Claude in a fit of

exuberance threw my father overboard - for which Nona never forgave him. My father's sole recollection of Claude was when he shot a snake and threw it, still writhing, at his two year old feet.

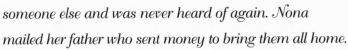

Unfortunately Claude wearied of Nona, ran off with someone else and was never heard of again. Nona mailed her father who sent money to bring them all home.

Her second husband was fifteen years her junior. An Irishman called Hoey Tuffnell-Barret he was always known as *Tuff*. He was 6 ft 5 inches tall and had a bushy moustache he was fond of twirling.

Inevitably this second marriage soured. News of *Tuff's* matrimonial escape arrived whilst Daddy was in the middle of a battle in Italy during WWII. Whilst bullets were flying a runner came up to him with an urgent telegram which read "*Tuff* run away. Go immediately and bring him back".

On Daddy's homecoming in 1945 Nona's first comment was "the one time I ask you to do something for me - you fail me". At this point in Daddy's favourite story he rolls his eyes to the heavens and mutters "I could have stuck a knife in her!"

There was only one sighting of him after that time. Mimi was having tea in the Ritz when she bumped into *Tuff* who was with a rather plain girlfriend. Mimi made the mistake of recounting this to Nona - who said "how dare you mention that long streak of poison in front of me!"

Potato & Mushroom Gratin

(serves 6)

2 1/2 LBS WAXY POTATOES

1-2 LBS MUSHROOMS

1 CLOVE OF GARLIC

1 TBLSP BUTTER

4 TBLSP FINELY CHOPPED ONION

4 TBLSP CHOPPED PARSLEY

6 TBLSP GRATED GRUYERE CHEESE

1/2 PINT WHIPPING OR SINGLE CREAM

SALT AND PEPPER

Peel or scrub the potatoes and slice thinly. Slice the mushrooms not so thinly, and season both with salt & pepper. Rub a gratin dish with the garlic clove and butter. Alternate layers of potato and mushroom, sprinkling with the chopped onion, parsley and 4 tblsp of the cheese. Pour on the cream, scatter the remaining cheese over the dish and dot with butter. Cook in a preheated oven at 170°c, 325°f or Gas mark 3, for a total of 1 3/4 hours. Lower the temperature a little when the dish begins to bubble.

Roast Duck with Walnut Stuffing

(serves 4)

*M*imi adored all 'cute looking' things. She loved babies but not naughty children - fluffy ducklings were another of her favourites. However, her immense regard for good food meant that grown up ducklings had to watch out !

1 MEDIUM-SIZED DUCK

The Stuffing

2 LARGE EATING APPLES - CORED AND DICED

3/4 LB BELLY OF PORK, MINCED

1 LARGE CLOVE OF GARLIC, CRUSHED

2 OZ CHOPPED WALNUTS	**1 TBLSP CHOPPED PARSLEY**
4 OZ BREADCRUMBS	**1 DSP HONEY**
4 OZ CHOPPED ONION	**1 LARGE EGG**
2 OZ BUTTER	**SALT AND PEPPER**

*Gently fry the onions, garlic, apples and minced
pork in the butter gently for 15 minutes.
Mix with all the other ingredients
to make the stuffing.*

Stuff into the duck...

Roast the Duck...

Place the duck in a roasting tin and prick it all over
with a skewer (quite deeply to let the fat run out).
Roast the duck in a hot oven, at 220°c, 425°f or
Gas mark 7, for the first 20 minutes.
Then reduce heat to 180°c, 350°f or Gas mark 4,
for the remainder of the roasting time.
You will need to roast the duck for a total of
30 minutes per pound, draining the fat occasionally.

This is absolutely delicious
served with the following sauce.

Salsa Victoria

(an excellent sauce for roast duck or venison)

3 TBLSP BLACKCURRANT JELLY

I CUP OF PORT OR SHERRY   **I TSP CAYENNE PEPPER**

I CUP OF GOOD STOCK   **I CINNAMON STICK**

I ORANGE   **3 CLOVES**

Melt the blackcurrant jelly over a low heat,
add the port or sherry and the stock.
Grate the rind from the orange and add it
along with the cinnamon stick and cloves.
Simmer for a little while
and just before serving
add the juice of the orange
and the cayenne pepper.

Serve separately in your best gravy boat
with the roast duck, roast potatoes and parsnips.

Portuguese Lamb with Lemon Sauce

(serves 4)

2 LB BEST END OF NECK OF LAMB

1 TBSP CHOPPED PARSLEY	**1 MEDIUM SIZE ONION**
3 OZ WALNUT KERNELS	**SALT**
GRATED RIND OF 1 LEMON	**BLACK PEPPER**
2 TBLSPS BUTTER	**1 1/2 OZ BREADCRUMBS**
1 SMALL BEATEN EGG	**1 GLASS OF WHITE WINE**

Bone the lamb, score the fat and season the surface of the meat with salt and pepper. Grind the nuts. Soften the onion in 1 tblsp of the butter and add with the remaining ingredients to the nuts. Mix to make a stuffing and spread over the inside of the meat. Roll up and fasten with poultry pins.

Place the meat in a roasting tin. Spread the outside of the joint with butter and pour over a glass of white wine. Roast in a hot oven for 20 minutes, (240°c, 475°f or Gas mark 9,) then turn down temperature to 220°c, 425°f or Gas mark 7 and roast for another 20-30 minutes. Baste well throughout. Meanwhile, make the lemon sauce...

Lemon sauce:

RIND AND JUICE OF 1/2 LEMON

1/4 PINT OF GOOD CLEAR STOCK

1/4 PINT OF WHITE WINE

1 TSP REDCURRANT JELLY

1 DSP CORNFLOUR

Pare lemon rind thinly and cut into shreds.
Blanch, drain and set aside. Mix the lemon juice
with the stock and wine in a saucepan.
Add the redcurrant jelly and bring to the boil,
stirring until the jelly is dissolved. Mix the cornflour
with a small amount of water and add to the
liquid in the pan, along with the lemon rind.
Just before serving, add the strained juices
from the roast lamb and serve whilst piping hot.

Yorkshire Rarebit

When Mimi wasn't 'trying to impress' she was equally happy settling down to an evening of Emmerdale Farm and a glass of Martini Rosso. She would follow this with something simple but substantial like Yorkshire Rarebit.

1 TBLSP OF MILK OR ALE   **1/4 TO 1/2 TSP OF MUSTARD**

2 OZ GRATED CHEESE   **CAYENNE PEPPER**

1/2 TBLSP BUTTER   **SALT**

DASH OR 2 OF WORCESTERSHIRE SAUCE

ROUNDS OF BUTTERED TOAST

*Melt the butter in a saucepan and add the milk
or ale, mustard, Worcestershire sauce and cheese.
This mixture only needs to be heated through,
so be sure not to overcook it.
Season with a pinch of cayenne pepper and salt,
pour over the rounds of hot buttered toast,
sit down with your feet up
and relax!*

Hot Toddies

8 pm on Friday nights would see us clasping our hot toddies in the drawing room watching ghoulish stories from the 'Hammer House of Horror'.

Mimi would prepare by turning all the lights off and then settle back in her favourite green velvet armchair in front of the flickering TV. I would sit at her feet on my little tapestry stool where she would rhythmically scratch my scalp with her clear polished nails. As the action started I'd scream and hide my face behind cushions but I cannot remember one instance where Mimi showed any signs of unease.

The one particular episode still with me today concerned a man who argued with his wife and proceeded to bury her alive in the garden. What disturbed me most was the scenes of worms and other creepy crawlies clambering over her trapped body. It reminded me of a recurring

dream where I was being forced to watch my mother's
coffin being exhumed. On seeing her again she bore a
close resemblance to Howard Hughes with hair down
to her waist and nails about 5 inches long. Endless
variations of these images multiplied in my mind and for
about six months afterwards I suffered terrible nightmares
at home causing my parents many broken nights.

Nonetheless when staying with Mimi, we continued our
regular Friday night routine. As I snuggled up to her in
bed she'd croon in my ear "Slumber in the bosom of your
old mama genie, Briar Fox will catch you if you don't".

Hot Toddy

4 PARTS WHISKY

1 PART LEMON JUICE

3 DASHES ANGOSTURA BITTERS

2 DASHES HONEY

5 PARTS BOILING WATER

Mimi's Sweet Tooth

always led to a
sticky ending

One thing Mimi couldn't be trusted with was sweets. If I ever had a stash at hand, she would insist on looking after them under some tooth or appetite saving pretext. This often happened in the darkness of Chelsea cinema ("Pass those caramels to me children, before you drop them").

We shared a large four poster bed with Mimi. Putting us to bed she would say in her heavily accented English "Sweets are so bad for you dahhlings - never to be eaten after brushing your teeth". How was it then that I heard the crackling of paper during the night from Mimi's side of the bed and why did my jellies always disappear? It was this constant advice along with childlike naughtiness that endeared her to everyone..

Banana Icecream

(serves 6)

*H*elping Mimi make icecream in her small
kitchen in Tedworth Square was always fun.
Unfortunately I could never wait until the mixture
was frozen - 3 or 4 hours might just as well have
been 3 or 4 years to me, it seemed such an eternity.

sticky endings

3/4 PINT SINGLE CREAM	1 DSP LEMON JUICE
PINCH OF SALT	2 RIPE BANANAS
2 OZ SUGAR	2 EGGS

Scald the cream but do not boil.

Stir in the sugar and salt and leave to get cold.

Beat the eggs (yolks & whites) until stiff
and fold into the cooled cream.

Pour into a freezing tray and freeze until mushy.

Slice the bananas thinly into a bowl, mash them
to a pulp with a fork and press through a sieve.

Stir in the lemon juice and 1 tsp of the sugar.

Turn the frozen cream and egg mixture into a
chilled bowl and beat in the banana juice
with an egg whisk until blended.

Return the mixture to the freezing tray
and freeze until hard (about 3 - 4 hours.)

Serve with sponge fingers or slices of lightly toasted
sponge cake. A little rum is a pleasant addition.

Prince Charles' Pancakes

(serves 6)

Mimi was always sceptical about my father's lineage. Her favourite aside was "if he wore a turban he could pass for an Indian". She did, however, share his love of anything rich and sweet.

The title of this dish also gave Mimi an opportunity to assume unfounded royal connections.

sticky endings

The Batter

4 oz Plain Flour   **1/2 Pint of Milk**

2 Beaten Eggs   **Pinch of Salt**

The Sauce

3 Large Oranges   **4 oz Castor Sugar**

2 Large Lemons   **3 oz Butter**

3 tblsp Drambuie or Whisky

*Gradually add the beaten eggs and milk
to the flour and salt, whisking to make a batter.
Make into pancakes and keep them warm.
Grate the rind from the oranges and lemons
and squeeze out the juice.
Melt the butter, stir in the sugar
and cook for 1 minute, then add grated rinds,
orange and lemon juices and bring to the boil.
Add the Drambuie or whisky and
simmer for 3 minutes. Spoon the sauce over the
pancakes and serve immediately.*

Walnut Pie

(serves 6-8)

Guests would always comment about how much time and trouble Mimi must have taken to shell the walnuts without breaking them.

Of course she bought them pre-shelled, but true to form wouldn't have dreamt of disappointing them with the truth.

Shortcrust Pastry

8 oz Plain Flour   **2 tblsp Icing Sugar**

5 oz Butter   **1 Egg Yolk**

about 1 tblsp Water

The Filling

4oz Soft Brown Sugar   **8 oz Shelled Walnuts**

4oz Unsalted Butter   **6 oz Golden Syrup**

3 Eggs   **Pinch of Salt.**

Juice and Zest of 1 Lemon

First make the pastry

Rub the butter into the flour and icing sugar.

Add the egg yolk and then enough water

to make a pliable pastry.

Line an 8 1/2 or 9 1/2 inch removable base tart tin with

the pastry and bake blind for 5 minutes

at 200°c, 400°f or Gas mark 6.

For the filling

Cream together the butter and sugar until light.

Beat in the eggs one at a time.

Warm the syrup and mix into the butter

and sugar mixture. Add the walnuts,

lemon juice, lemon zest and a pinch of salt.

Turn into the pre-baked pastry case.

Bake for about 3/4 hour at 180°c, 350°f or Gas mark 4,

until the filling is lightly browned and risen.

Serve with single cream or crème fraiche.

Caramel Baked Pears

(serves 4 - 6)

Quick and easy to make this recipe has a smooth, melt-in-the-mouth quality. Its richness is not for the faint hearted and is best eaten on a cold winter evening or after a day outdoors.

6 ANJOU PEARS

(OR ANOTHER VARIETY IF THESE ARE NOT AVAILABLE)

4 TBLSP OF BROWN SUGAR

4 TBLSP OF BUTTER

HEAVY CREAM OR SOUR CREAM TO SERVE

Peel and quarter the pears,
and place in a shallow baking dish.
Sprinkle with the sugar and dot with the butter.
Put in a hot oven, (220°c, 425°f or Gas mark 7)
and bake until the sugar is brown and caramelised.
Serve warm with the cream poured over the top.

Traditional Custard

When we were little Mimi used to go to great trouble making a proper custard, with eggs and all the fresh ingredients. However we all thought it disgusting and preferred it made with Bird's custard powder. This made her laugh.

1/2 PINT OF DOUBLE OR SINGLE CREAM

3 EGG YOLKS

1 TBLSP CASTER SUGAR

1 TSP CORNFLOUR

2 DROPS OF VANILLA ESSENCE

Blend the egg yolks, cornflour,
sugar and vanilla essence in a mixing bowl.
Heat the cream up until just boiling,
and pour into the mixture, stirring all the time.
Return the mixture to the saucepan
and heat gently until the sauce has thickened.

Breakfast
in bed

As she grew older Mimi seemed to sleep more soundly and would need to be awakened most mornings. I would take breakfast in to her on a tray at around 8am. Mimi's bedroom was small but bright and sunny and warmly decorated in yellow with deep crimson accents. Breakfast consisted of a small pot of Earl Grey tea and one slice of buttered toast. As she tucked in, her first advice of the day was usually "one slice is fine for you dahhling, two slices makes you fat!" Followed by "If I don't watch my figure nobody else will".After delivering these weighty statements she would put on her glasses and read the Daily Mail with much tut tutting and enjoyment over the most scandalous stories. An hour later she would be ready to get dressed.

Mimi wore underwear like armour as if she might come under attack from a marauding male at any moment. She called bras 'bust bodices' and had a penchant for corsets that shrank with a snapping sound when she took them off in the evening. From the waist down to the top of her thighs was referred to as the 'nether region' and not talked about. However it was quite respectable to show off her slim ankles. She wore ultra sheer stockings. I remember peeling them off her legs, careful to avoid laddering them when she got too frail to do it herself.

Baked Lemon Tart

(serves 6)

The Pastry

6 oz Plain Flour   **3oz Butter**

1 Egg Yolk   **pinch of Salt**

1 heaped tblsp Icing Sugar

The Filling

Juice of 2 Lemons   **4 oz Castor Sugar**

Grated Zest of 1 Lemon   **3oz Double Cream**

4 Egg Yolks   **2oz Ground Almonds**

4 oz Unsalted Butter, Softened

First make the pastry

Rub the butter into the flour, salt and icing sugar.

Add the egg yolk and then enough water

to make a pliable pastry.

Line an 8 1/2 or 9 1/2 inch tart tin with a removable

base with the pastry and bake blind for 5 minutes

at 200°c, 400°f or Gas mark 6.

For the filling

Cream together the butter and sugar until light.

Add the eggs yolks, followed by the lemon juice,

lemon zest and ground almonds. Beat well.

Finally, add the cream and pour into the pastry case.

Bake for 30 - 40 minutes at 170°c, 325°f

or Gas mark 3, until slightly risen

and the pastry is nicely brown.

Serve with single cream.

Bakewell Tart

(serves 6)

*I*n 1947 when my mother was in her early
twenties Mimi returned to Chile to visit her
relatives for the first time in 36 years. On her return
by boat my grandfather couldn't believe his eyes
when he saw how much weight she had put on. It
then emerged that she had wrapped herself in layer
upon layer of beautiful antique lace bought for my
mother's wedding dress and had stacked her pill box
hat with silver plates. All this subterfuge was totally
unnecessary. She had been given diplomatic privileges
by a childhood friend of hers, Alessandri, who was
President of Chile at that time. She used to joke that
he had constantly asked her to marry him but she
could never trust him as he cheated in school exams.
I can only think that Mimi went to such trouble
purely for the thrill of it!

sticky endings

Her last trip to Chile was in the early seventies to pay her last respects to her mother who was one hundred and three at the time. She needn't have bothered as the old lady upon seeing Mimi said; "You're not my daughter. My daughter had long blonde plaits and was beautiful". The trip was not without some success however as Mimi managed to extract some of her mother's prized recipes - amongst them this delicious recipe for Bakewell tart.

The Pastry

6 OZ PLAIN FLOUR	**PINCH OF SALT**
I EGG YOLK	**I 1/2 OZ ICING SUGAR**
3 OZ UNSALTED BUTTER	**I TBLSP OF WATER**

The Filling

I TSP ALMOND ESSENCE	**2 OZ SOFTENED BUTTER**
2 YOLKS AND I EGG WHITE	**2 OZ GROUND ALMONDS**
2 OZ CASTOR SUGAR	**GOOD RASPBERRY JAM**

FLAKED ALMONDS TO SPRINKLE ON TOP

First make the pastry

Even Mimi would take short cuts if the results proved worthwhile. The easiest way to make this pastry is to put all the ingredients into a food processor. Once it forms a dough, knead the pastry gently then place in the fridge for half an hour while you make the filling.

For the filling

Cream the softened butter and sugar together until thick and white. Gradually stir in the egg yolks and egg white. Add the ground almonds and almond essence and beat well.

Roll out the pastry and line an 8 or 9 inch tart tin. Spread a good layer of raspberry jam over the base of the pastry and add the filling lightly over the top. Sprinkle with flaked almonds and bake in the oven at 170⁰c, 325⁰f or Gas mark 3 for about half an hour or until pale brown and nicely risen.

*A*t weekends I helped Mimi bake cakes and puddings in her small kitchen in Tedworth Square.

We took it in turns to beat the butter and sugar, holding the bowl on our laps to help soften the mixture. Although Mimi didn't take any formal exercise her wrists were unbelievably strong. I always gave up after a minute or so and was more intent on stealing dabs of raw mixture whilst she bent down to check the oven temperature.

She would then chide me saying I was too impatient and greedy to make a good cook.

Batatada

Sweet potato mash

(serves 4 - 6)

Whilst the creamy texture of this recipe is reminiscent of baby food it makes a surprisingly sophisticated dessert when served with fresh cream and a dusting of cinnamon.

8 OZ SWEET POTATOES, PEELED AND BOILED

5 OZ GRANULATED SUGAR

1/4 PINT OF WATER

8 EGG YOLKS

CREAM AND CINNAMON TO SERVE

Boil the potatoes until soft. Meanwhile make a syrup by dissolving the sugar in the water, and simmering for a few minutes. Mash the potatoes, add the syrup mixture and simmer vigorously for about 10 minutes, or until it thickens slightly. Allow to cool. Stir in the egg yolks one by one, and cook gently until the mixture thickens - when you can divide it with a spoon. This doesn't take very long, but you need to stir it constantly. Chill before serving.

Never too old to *Flirt*

As she grew older and frailer Mimi was prone to falls.

The only fall I actually witnessed occurred as she stepped forward to shake hands with my Aunt Jan's nephew, a beautiful part time model from Australia. She insisted he carry her back upstairs where, after a restorative drink, she recovered.

For a long time afterwards Mimi would muse to anyone who would listen about how he scooped her up in his strong arms "like a bride" and that his arms "were like tree trunks dahhling".

Paulita's Walnut Cake

(a traditional Chilean dessert)

*J*ust after the war Mimi employed a top Austrian restaurant chef, luring her away from more prestigious establishments with an audacious live in wage of twenty-five shillings a week, which was five times the going rate. She was desperate to learn her techniques and recipes but the response was always "No Madam, professionals don't give their secrets away". After a frustrating two months Mimi felt forced to let the stubborn chef go.

However, she had no difficulty in squeezing culinary secrets from her nearest and dearest. The following exquisite recipe belongs to Paulita, one of her Chilean cousins.

sticky endings

8 oz Icing Sugar

8 oz Coarsely Ground Walnuts

1 tblsp Baking Powder

2 oz Plain Flour   **1 cup Whipped Cream**

7 Eggs   **2 -3 tblsps Whisky**

for the meringue topping

6 oz Caster Sugar

3 Egg Whites

2 oz Coarsely Ground Walnuts

Whisk the seven whole eggs until frothy, then add sifted icing sugar and ground walnuts one spoonful at a time, whisking as you go. Lastly add the flour and baking powder sifted together. Beat the mixture slowly with a wooden spoon until bubbles appear on the surface. Spoon into a greased and floured 10" round cake tin. Add a layer of whipped cream, the extra 2 oz ground walnuts and sprinkle over the whisky. Make the meringue topping by whisking the egg whites until very stiff, then gradually whisk in the sugar. Spread over the cake mixture and bake in a preheated oven for 45 minutes at 170⁰c, 325⁰f or Gas mark 3, or until the sponge is cooked.

"Your Last Night on Earth"

Like our father and Uncle before him Ian was sent to Harrow which thrilled Mimi no end. There he flourished at sport and had many friends. He was a sweet shy boy and was as Mimi would put it a 'late developer' with regard to girls.

At around 15 he was invited to a party in London by a fellow Harrovian and was told to bring a partner. This last request filled him with consternation. He scoured his mind for someone to invite and Mimi and I were drawn into targeting a suitable girl. Julie was a childhood friend of mine who had had a crush on Ian for as long as I could remember. Not to be outdone I had a crush on her brother and together we planned our joint wedding! Thrilled with the role of matchmaker I planned the evening down to the minutest detail, bossing poor Julie on what she should wear and what she should and shouldn't say. "Imagine" I said "that this is your last night on earth and you're going to make the most of it". Mimi and I waved her off at the front door and spent a cozy evening with a TV dinner. Next morning I went downstairs to the guest room to awaken Julie. Between tears she told me what happened. Ian had played 'hide' without the 'seek' with Julie all evening. He had introduced her to no one and turned his back on her throughout the party. For a whole week I sent Ian to coventry. I don't think he minded much, preferring silence to confrontation but he couldn't totally escape Mimi's tut tutting over his ungentlemanly behaviour.

As he grew older an endless stream of my girlfriends fell under his spell. They would trot round to his flat on Saturday evenings whilst he watched Match of the Day, not only cooking his meals, but washing up as well. They were lucky if he bothered to wave them off at the door.

Mimi was horrified. In her day men were expected to be entertaining to the ladies and she couldn't understand why young women had to try so hard to catch a man.

A trip to Harrods on Saturday morning was one of the highlights of our weekend with Mimi. Dressing up for this event was all important. In winter she would wear a fur coat, hat and a veil. Then *A trip to Harrods.* we would walk the fifteen minutes down the Kings Road to Peter Jones and along Sloane Street to this world famous store. After an appetite whetting foray into the food hall we would make our way to the tea room on the fifth floor. Rushing towards the sweet trolley we would be allowed to choose a cake. Mimi was always loyal in her choice of a Danish pastry and a cup of Earl Grey tea. Mission accomplished, we would walk back home and before long would be discussing what delicacies to eat next.

...and other sweet stories

High Tee

Mimi was never known for her prowess in sport. The only time she flirted with the idea was when social aspiration got the better of her.

In the late fifties William became a member of the prestigious Moore Park golf club in North London. Mimi splashed out on full golfing regalia and William bought her a set of clubs. She played no more than twice. William's Scottish soul was mortified at this wanton extravagance. As a peace offering Mimi took to bringing scones and strawberry jam to the club house on Saturday afternoons.

Scones

(makes 12)

12 oz Plain Flour   2 tblsp Caster Sugar

1 1/2 oz Butter   1 Egg

1 1/2 tsp Baking Powder

about 1/4 pt Milk (Sour Milk is Best)

Sift the flour and baking powder together in a mixing
bowl. Rub in the butter, stir in sugar and mix well.
Break the egg into a cup. Take about 1/2 a teaspoon
of the yolk and mix with 2 tsps of the milk.
Put to one side for polishing the tops of the scones
later. Beat the remaining egg and mix into the dry
ingredients, along with enough milk to form a nice
soft dough. Roll out evenly to just over 1/2 inch thick
and cut into rounds with a metal cutter.
Place on a greased baking sheet and brush the tops
with reserved egg and milk mixture.
Bake for about 15 minutes or until pale brown,
at 220°c, 425°f or Gas mark 7.
Delicious with jam and clotted cream,
or Mimi's lemon curd.

Strawberry Jam

(makes about 3 jars)

3LBS SMALL STRAWBERRIES

2 LBS CASTER SUGAR

THE JUICE OF TWO LARGE LEMONS

Make sure the strawberries are dry. Remove the stalks and put the fruit into a preserving pan or very large saucepan in alternate layers with the sugar. Leave overnight. The next day add the lemon juice and put the pan over a low heat until the sugar has dissolved, stirring to prevent burning. When the sugar has dissolved bring slowly to the boil, and from then on boil rapidly for about 20 to 30 minutes. While this is boiling, put a couple of saucers in the freezer ready to test for jam setting. At 20 minutes test for a set by trying a little on a cold plate to see if it a skin forms. If not, put back to boil and test every 3 - 4 minutes until set. Once set, leave the jam to cool for 15 minutes, then put into warmed jars and cover.

Spread and enjoy on freshly baked scones or bread.

Lemon Curd

2 oz Butter

1 oz Margarine

2 Lemons

2 Eggs

3 oz Caster Sugar

Put the juice of 2 lemons and the grated zest

of 1 lemon into a double saucepan,

together with the butter, margarine and sugar.

Heat until melted.

Add the well beaten eggs and stir frequently

over gently simmering heat until thick.

This takes about 20 minutes.

Be careful not to let it boil.

Leave to cool, stirring now and again.

(It will thicken more when cold).

Fills one medium-sized jar.

Keep in the refrigerator, if it lasts that long!

Cut & Come Again Cake

This cake which improves with keeping was a great favourite of Mimi's. Rich and moist in texture it's calorific - but since Mimi equated slenderness with poverty this was no cause for alarm. It does take time to make, but a slice of this cake is so satisfying that it's always worth the effort.

and again until....

5 oz Self Raising Flour

Pinch of Salt   **4 oz Butter**

3/4 lb Mixed Dry Fruit   **4 oz Castor Sugar**

2 oz Glace Cherries   **2 Eggs**

I oz Chopped Mixed Peel   **4 fl ozs Carnation Milk**

Sieve together the flour and add the dried fruit,
cherries and mixed peel.
Cream the butter and sugar until pale and fluffy
and gradually add the beaten eggs.
With a metal spoon carefully fold in the fruit
and flour alternately with the carnation milk.
Turn into an 8 inch cake tin lined with
grease-proof paper and bake in a preheated oven
at 150⁰c, 300⁰f or Gas mark 2, for about 2 hours or
until a skewer stuck into the cake comes out clean.
This cake is rich enough as is, but is also lovely
glazed with marmalade if you have some handy.

Soda Bread

1LB 6OZ WHOLEMEAL FLOUR

12 OZ WHITE FLOUR

2 TSP SUGAR

1 1/2 TSP SALT

1 SMALL JAR OF NATURAL YOGURT

2 TSP BICARBONATE OF SODA

FEW DROPS LEMON JUICE

1 1/2 OZ BUTTER

APPROX 1 PT MILK

In a large mixing bowl rub the butter
into the flours thoroughly and lightly.
Mix in the bicarbonate of soda, salt and sugar.
Add the milk and yogurt gradually
to make a dough, finishing with a
few drops of lemon juice.
Shake some flour on your board and hands,
shape the dough into a round and place it on a
baking sheet. Sprinkle with a little more flour
and bake in the oven for about 50 - 60 minutes
at 190⁰c, 375⁰f or Gas mark 5, until risen
and hollow sounding when tapped.
Makes one big round loaf.

Mis de Sola

(Date cake)

1 1/4 tsp Bicarbonate of Soda

1 cup Chopped Dates	**1 Egg**
3/4 cup Boiling Water	**scant tsp of Salt**
3/4 cup of Brown Sugar	**1 tsp Vanilla Essence**
1 1/2 cups of Flour	**1/4 cup Melted Butter**

Cut up dates and place in a bowl.
Add the bicarbonate of soda and pour the boiling
water over the top. Leave to cool.
Beat the egg and sugar until light and foamy.
Add the vanilla essence followed by the dates.
Fold the sifted flour into the mixture and then add
the melted butter. Pour into a 7 inch deep cake tin
and bake for 50 minutes in a preheated oven
at 170°c, 325°f or Gas mark 3,
until the sponge is light and springy.

Home Helps

Mimi belonged to an era where home helps and nannies were an essential part of life. At Tedworth square Norah looked after Mimi's flat and Gladys (always referred to as Mrs Neale) looked after Jan and Colin in their flat upstairs. I never once heard them refer to each other by name. They were just known as 'her upstairs' and 'her down there'. Norah was an Irish Catholic with an unfathomable accent. She had a round maternal figure and enjoyed an easy familiar relationship with Mimi. Mrs Neale, on the other hand was a formidable character. Though we all knew her for over twenty years none of us were ever on first name terms. She was working class, honest and proud. Her unremarkable face was topped with electrified hair dyed a variety of colours that would change almost weekly. It was sprayed so firmly into place that it seemed made of corrugated iron - rather like Mrs Neale herself. She had no eyebrows except those she haphazardly drew. To compensate for this she would make up her eyes in bright dramatic colours. On her thin mouth she wore a slash of red lipstick from which a cigarette hung precariously.

When Norah retired and we moved to Onslow Gardens Mrs Neale had us all under her beady eye. Anxious not to be the recipient of her sharp tongue there would be a mad flurry of activity before her arrival at 11.00am. At this time she must have been approaching seventy but she seemed as indestructible as ever. If I was home from university we would often share a coffee and I would nod my head too nervous to disagree as she rasped her usual litany of dissatisfaction with life. Subjects ranged from the abysmal state of London buses and their multiracial drivers to the state of her health.

Probably the greatest thing we had in common was our mutual love of Malibu which she would buy me every year for Christmas with precise instructions to mix it with pineapple juice. Her attempts to woo Mimi over proved futile and she remained staunchly loyal to Martini Rosso. However, Mimi wooed Mrs Neale into her style of dressing and there were many times I would freeze in my tracks as I caught sight of a figure in the street wearing one of Mimi's fur coats topped with bright aubergine hair.

Rich Chocolate Cake

*T*he only recipe that Mimi kept hidden away
from her black loose-leaf recipe folder was her
Rich Chocolate Cake. It was served for 4 o'clock tea
on an enamel cake stand in the drawing room. Mimi
basked in the attention as her guests marvelled at
its richness and speculated over the ingredients.
"Chocolate cake with a touch of class" she said.
"Class is a mystery, class cannot be defined". But to
us children chocolate cake was a gift to be eaten as
quickly as possible, no questions asked.

4oz Butter	**4 Eggs, Separated**
4oz Caster Sugar	**8oz Plain Chocolate**
Zest of 1/2 an Orange	**4oz Ground Almonds**
Zest of 1/2 a Lemon	**1 dsp of Brandy**
Icing Sugar to Dust	

Melt the chocolate, sugar and butter in a bowl
over a pan of boiling water. Transfer to a larger
mixing bowl and stir in the brandy,
lemon and orange zest and ground almonds.
Now beat in the egg yolks, one at a time.
Beat the egg whites until stiff.
Gently fold the whites into the chocolate mixture,
and pour into a well greased and floured 8" loaf tin.
Bake in a preheated oven, (180⁰c, 350⁰f
or Gas mark 4,) for 40 - 50 minutes,
or until a skewer comes out clean.
Let the cake cool in the tin before turning out
onto a posh plate and dusting with icing sugar.
Absolutely delicious by itself or with whipped cream
and strawberries for extra indulgence.

Meanwhile....

*Mrs Neale
was making
her own
Chocolate Cake.*

Mrs Neale's Chocolate Cake

When we were visiting Mimi on her own she knew that the subtleties and expense of her rich chocolate cake would be wasted on us. It was time for *Mrs. Neales Chocolate Cake* !

This delicious recipe with its smooth buttery icing and crunchy Smartie top tasted better than anything else we knew.

1 1/3 CUPS SELF-RAISING FLOUR **1/3 CUP HOT WATER**
1/3 CUP PLAIN FLOUR **8 OZ BUTTER**
1/3 CUP COCOA **10 OZ DARK CHOCOLATE**
1 CUP CASTER SUGAR **3 EGGS**

Butter Icing
4OZ UNSALTED BUTTER
8 OZ DARK CHOCOLATE
2 TBSP WHIPPED CREAM

Sift flours and cocoa into a large mixing bowl. Combine sugar, butter, chocolate and water in a medium pan. Stir over a low heat until melted and dissolved. Remove from heat and add to the flour mixture, stirring with a wooden spoon until just combined - do not overbeat. Pour into a deep 8" cake tin lined with greaseproof paper and bake for 1 1/2 hours in a preheated oven at 170°c, 325°f or Gas mark 3, or until cooked.

finishing the cake...

Combine icing ingredients in a small pan and stir over a low heat until melted. Remove from heat, cool and spread over the cooled cake - don't forget the Smarties or another decoration of your choice!

Time for Tea

Though Mimi would never have said possessions were the most important thing in life she loved to have beautiful things around her. Tea was the highlight of her day where her sweet tooth could be fully indulged and would always be served in fine china and elegant silver. I have inherited from her the most exquisite silver teaspoon set, each spoon representing a different flower - I can remember thinking as a child that they were too beautiful to use. But for Mimi "keeping a good table" was the hallmark of respectability and any hint of stinginess was a sign of "coming down in the world".

So there was always a wide choice of cakes and biscuits on offer - simnel cake, three tier chocolate cake, date cake, all of which would have caused deep anxiety to anyone coming to tea with a weight problem.

My return to the house for the 4 o'clock ritual was sacrosanct. Many was the day when as a thoughtless teenager I would forget the time. Arriving later than expected I would be greeted by the sound of rattling china in the kitchen marking Mimi's frustration at my forgetfulness.

Rebecca Graeber and I were firm friends at school. Both overweight we spent most of our free time wondering what was for lunch or dinner.

I had learned from Mimi that avocados and a second piece of toast were fattening but afternoon cakes were part of a healthy diet.

Firm Friends

At the beginning and end of each school term we endured an outmoded ritual of weighing for our school reports. As I stood on the scales I never felt depressed because I knew Rebecca would weigh in at least half a stone heavier.

OUT OF ORDER

She was an easy going girl and with her parents in Germany would often come and spend her exeats with me in Charing village, Kent. One weekend my parents went away leaving us a strict list of do's and don'ts on the kitchen table. Rebecca and I had other plans - a jaunt to Harrow, my brother's school, to harpoon a male or two!

We wobbled off to Charing station on decrepit bicycles and after two long train rides arrived at Harrow on the Hill feeling very defiant. By the time we had negotiated the school gates, endless corridors, found Ian's door and knocked we had just about run out of courage. Ian's greeting was no more than a curt whisper and a look that betrayed his fear of being caught with two fatties by his classmates.

So ten minutes had hardly elapsed before Rebecca and I were walking back down the hill, deflated, to the station. Not to be totally outdone, as our train pulled away from the platform we bared our breasts to a stunned group of Harrovians.

Russell's Uncooked Chocolate Cake

*M*avis, my father's sister, would sometimes come to visit us with her pet squirrel named Russell. He was a red squirrel purchased from Harrods animal department in the days when you could buy virtually anything there. He was a great character and used to climb up on the clothes hanging behind the door, bite off all the buttons and throw them on the floor.

Mimi would be horrified to see Mavis arrive with the mischievous squirrel in tow. One evening she cooked an elaborate supper and treated us to her favourite after dinner chocolate treat. No sooner were they placed on the table when Russell, sharing our sweet tooth, suddenly leapt into the middle of the plate. Stuffing delicacies into his pouches he shot off around the room looking for a suitable caché.

Russell showed great taste in petit fours, as the following recipe is bursting with nuts, fruit and the best quality chocolate.

4 oz Mixed Nuts (Almonds, Walnuts, Hazelnuts)

4 oz Chopped Candied Peel

6 oz Butter	**2 Eggs**
8 oz 'Nice' Biscuits	**8 oz Plain Chocolate**
2 oz Glace Cherries	**3 oz Castor Sugar**
3 oz Seedless Raisins	**3-4 tblsp Sherry or Brandy**

Put the biscuits into a paper bag and with a rolling
pin smash into crumbs. Chop the nuts and cut the
cherries into quarters. Mix with the crumbs,
the raisins and the chopped candied peel.
Put the chocolate, butter, sugar and eggs into a bowl
over simmering water and stir until the chocolate
has melted. Add the sherry or brandy
and stir into the dry mixture until well blended.
Pour the mixture into a loose bottomed tin and
refrigerate until hard. Cut into small squares and
keep refrigerated until ready to serve.

Serve after dinner, and watch out for squirrels!

Boyfriend Blues

It wasn't until I turned nineteen that I had my first serious boyfriend. With his pushiness and lack of finesse Jerome was a complete contrast to my expectations of romance but I was anxious to kick off my first relationship.

We met whilst studying French at Lille University before starting our degree in the U.K.

His French mother had been killed in a car crash when he was eight. Brought up by his father in Esher, Surrey he hadn't seen his mother's family since childhood.

When he invited me to visit his grandmother for the weekend in Fontainebleau I didn't hesitate to accept. Grandmothers, to my mind, were appealing and safe.

We shot down from Lille in his red Vauxhall Astra and it wasn't until just outside Fontainebleau that he informed me that since there was no room at his grandmother's house she had booked us into a hotel nearby.

On meeting her, any preconceived ideas of her resemblance to Mimi or anybody elses' grandmother flew straight out the window. At 60 she was tall and slim with red hair piled into an elegant chignon. This elegance was coupled with an open mindedness that gave me a sinking feeling during dinner which I couldn't shake off.

She escorted us herself to the hotel and bade us 'bon rêves' as she turned on her refined heel and left us. Faced with a double bed the guarding of my virginity seemed bleak. Jerome gallantly offered to place a bolster down the centre of the bed and though this worked for the first night I capitulated on the second. The next morning I felt depressed. Seeking comfort I phoned Emma in London who still had hers to lose. Meanwhile on my return home I was anxious to get Mimi's approval of at least part of my excursion with Jerome. Sitting in her kitchen munching on her welcome home meal I showed her a photograph of over exuberant boys in a red golf GTI. "Mimi guess which one is my boyfriend". Pointing straight at him she replied "who is this one dahhling I don't like his face!".

A Girl's
Best Friend

For many years Mimi wore two sparkling
diamond rings. Both were impressive, one a
solitaire and the other a gold band set with three large
diamonds. The solitaire was promised to me for my
twenty-first birthday and the other pledged to Ian and his
prospective bride.

Before going to bed Mimi would place both rings in a cut
glass jar with a silver top on her dressing table.

When her hands became too gnarled to wear them she
took them to her safety deposit box in Harrods. Arm in
arm we would leave the glare and bustle of the shop floor
for the quiet solemnity of the vaults. Mimi would whisper
her password through the grill and as if by magic a
heavy door would swing open. Next an old man with a
pronounced limp would usher us into a little cubicle where
the deposit box was placed on a table. We would both sit
on high stools and rummage through the jumbled up

jewellery, medals belonging to long dead relatives and miniature boxes filled with cuttings of children's hair.

When Ian announced his engagement Mimi retrieved his ring but declared that mine was missing. After a short search we all presumed Mimi had inadvertently thrown it away.

It wasn't until well after her death that we remembered Mimi's deposit box at Harrods. There, beyond the reach of her arthritic fingers and failing eyesight, concealed in a ball of cotton wool was my diamond ring. I wear the ring every day only taking it off for cleaning. Sometimes when I look at it I can't help but remember her advice; "Remember dahhling, you marry the lifestyle not the man."

Goodbye Mimi

After fracturing her hip in a fall Mimi spent her last months being cared for at home by a willowy blond nurse from New Zealand called Kim. With her pouty lips and black leather attire Kim was a ray of light at an otherwise gloomy time.

In March 1987 Mimi died aged eighty-nine. We all keenly felt the loss as she had been the central figure around whom our lives had revolved.

The funeral service took place in the Brompton Oratory where my parents had been married forty years earlier. It was a small gathering of family and close friends. Mrs Neale was there in one of Mimi's fur coats and with full makeup but thankfully without the ever-present cigarette. The priest arrived late and flustered. He gathered himself quickly and in a tone full of sympathy pronounced "It's particularly tragic when we lose our loved ones so young".

None of the living saw the funny side until later but I'm certain that lying between us in her frothy pink nightie Mimi was smiling and smiling.

sticky endings

and other sweet stories

thank you

*I would like to thank my original collaborators,
Simone, Nigel and Steve for all those evenings spent
cooking and eating inordinate amounts of food and
teasing out more stories over glasses of wine.*

*My cousins, the Chubretovich's and Berguño's for
translating and even amending Mimi's recipes
and to Diana for her help in translation.*

*My thanks also to Jan and Vivien for their
enthusiastic recipe testing and to my family
for inspiring some of the stories. Thanks also
to aunt Mavis for sharing her memories.*

*To Jon and Bronwen for taking a gamble on
a nervous would-be author found wandering
around a bookfair.*

*And finally my thanks to Mimi for stealing
my sweets and preserving my teeth at the
expense of her own.*

sprinkle
...és almonds pound...

Batatada [[Ca...

6 oz camotes pelados y coci...
5 oz azucar granulada
4 oz agua
9 yemas de huevos
Canela
4 oz crema y azucar
Se para los camotes por...
almibar claro con el agua...
con los camotes y se co...
enfria y se junta con...
sigue cocinando hasta...
con una cucharas Al u...
Listo y se pure con...